art for chi

figuring figures

by
Brigitte Baumbusch

Stewart, Tabori & Chang
NEW YORK

making a figure is easy

Jean Dubuffet, a French painter, drew his brightly colored figures with just a few lines, the way children do.

The two little figures above are signs that were used in ancient Chinese writing of two to three thousand years ago. They look like human figures, but who knows what they stand for?

This little girl with her toy animal was drawn in 1939 by the Swiss artist Paul Klee.

just a line or two

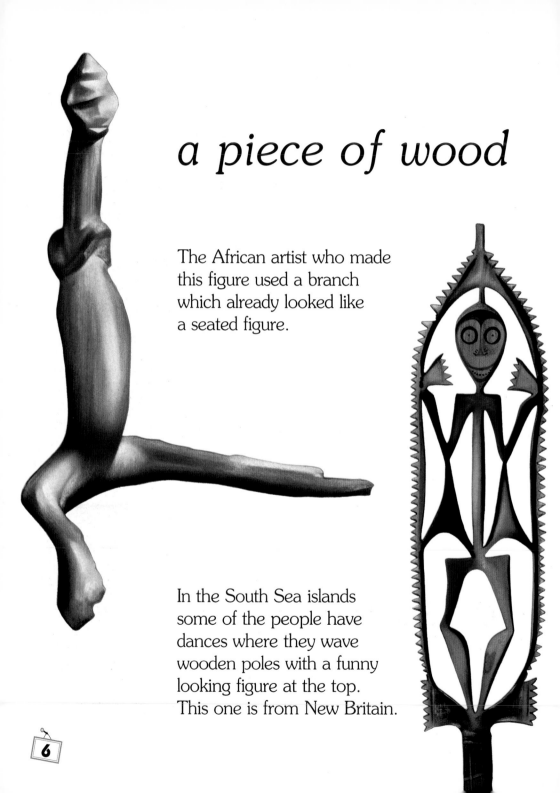

a piece of wood

The African artist who made
this figure used a branch
which already looked like
a seated figure.

In the South Sea islands
some of the people have
dances where they wave
wooden poles with a funny
looking figure at the top.
This one is from New Britain.

This is the silhouette
of an orchestra conductor.
A silhouette is made by
cutting a shape out of a piece
of black paper and mounting
it on a sheet of white paper.

or some paper

These crêche figurines are in painted terra cotta. They come from the South American Andes and are dressed just like the Indians who made them. The Christ Child is in a sort of pouch still used there to carry around little babies.

a bit of clay

or iron

This large figure in
iron represents the
god of war of the
Yoruba tribe in
Dahomey in Africa.
It might also be the
blacksmith god who
taught the Yoruba
how to work iron.

figures can be huge

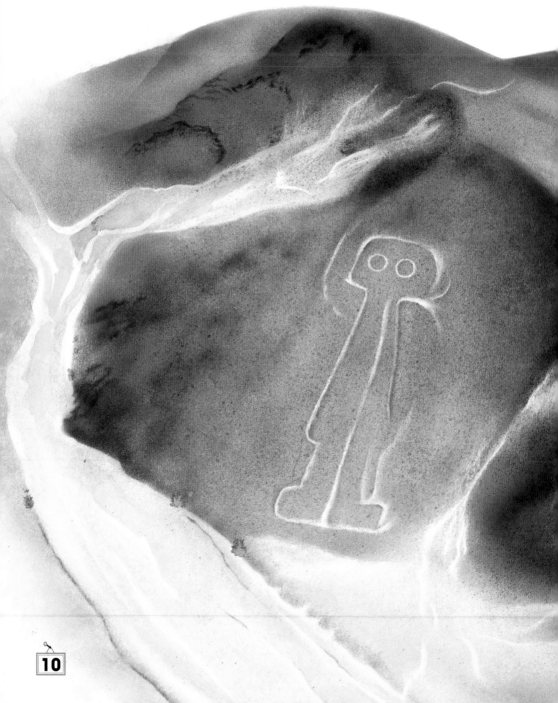

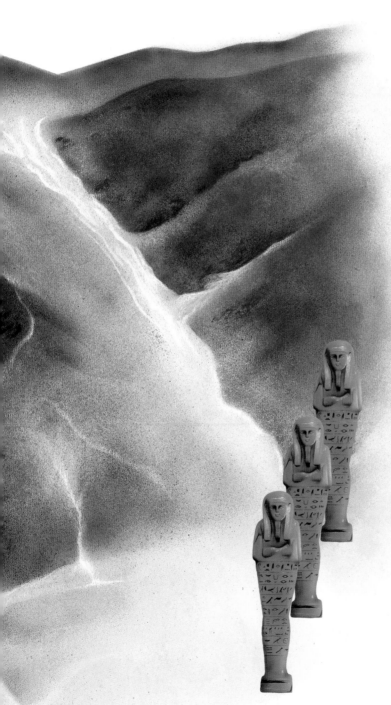

This huge outline of a human figure on an arid hillside in Peru was drawn by making grooves in the ground. It has been there now for over a thousand years.

The Egyptian statuette, on the other hand, is tiny, no more than eight inches high. Figurines like this, in the shape of a mummy, accompanied the pharaohs to their tombs so they would have servants in the next world.

or tiny

round as a *ball,*

or thin as a *rail,*

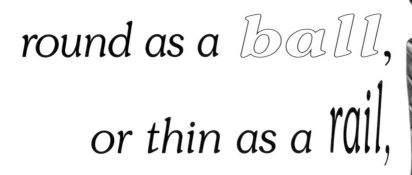

Both these figures come
from Mediterranean
countries and are more
or less the same age:
about 2,300
years old.

The terra cotta
"ball" was made
in Sardinia.
The bronze "rod"
was made by the
Etruscans who lived in
Italy before the Romans.

or made of cubes

The Italian artist who drew this scene of men fighting more than four centuries ago made the figures in cube shapes as if they were mannequins or robots.

in scale

In this figure of a man, set into a circle and also into a square, Leonardo da Vinci, one of the greatest Renaissance artists, wanted to show how the various parts of the human body related to each other in size.

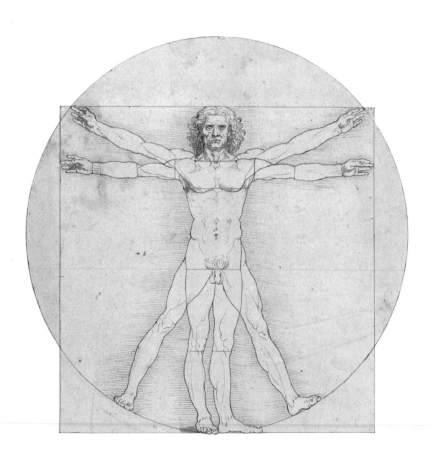

A long thin
man and a
short fat man
walk along
a street.
The American
artist Lyonel
Feininger
painted them
in the early
1900s.

or

out of

scale

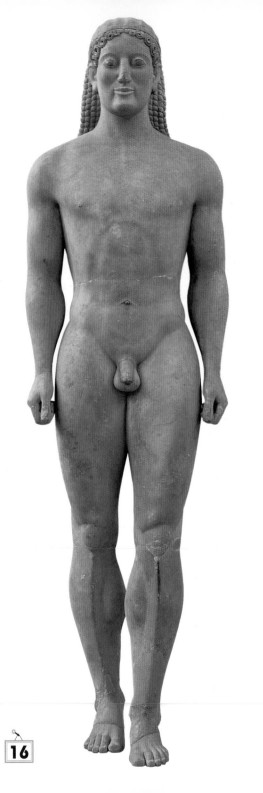

nude

This splendid marble statue of a handsome strong young man is a masterpiece of Greek art and was made more than 2,500 years ago. Showing people nude was one of the most natural things in the world for the Greeks and not a bit embarrassing or shameful.

This little girl painted in the seventeenth century by the Spaniard Diego Velazquez looks as if she has too many clothes on. She was a princess and this is why she had to be dressed in sumptuous dresses like the rich ladies of the court.

or dressed

figures are people

A husband and wife hold hands, perhaps to pray
in the temple. This little figurine was made
in the ancient land of Sumer in Mesopotamia
(now Iraq) around 4,500 years ago.

who can be by themselves

or with a lot of others

This garden crowded with children playing together was
painted by the Russian Kasimir Malevich in the early 1900s.

These four women running as fast as they can were painted on a rock in Australia in prehistoric times.

they may run

There is only one little girl running in this painting, but her movement is repeated over and over like in the frames of a film. It was made by the Italian painter Giacomo Balla early in the 1900s.

The bronze statue
of a seated man, deep
in thought, was made
by the French sculptor
Auguste Rodin more
than a hundred
years ago.

or stay
still

they dance

Both these
women seem
to be dancing the
same dance, but
one is ever so much
older than the other.

The figure at the
top was made by
a French woman,
Niki de Saint Phalle,
in 1965, and the
other one was
painted on a rock
in the Sahara
over 8,000
years ago.

On this page, Pulcinella figures have fun on a swing. (Pulcinella is a sort of clown in the Neapolitan comic theater.) The scene, seen from below, is by the Venetian painter Giandomenico Tiepolo, who lived in the eighteenth century.

and

play

sit down *and talk together*

The large painting is by the French painter Paul Gauguin. He painted it a hundred years ago when he was living on the island of Tahiti in the South Seas.

The two people shown below have stopped to sit and talk and were drawn on a rock in Chad, a country in Africa, almost 10,000 years ago.

TA MATETE

or lie down and sleep

This *Sleeping Lady* in terra cotta was
found in a temple on the island of Malta
and is over 5,000 years old.

The German
artist Erich
Heckel
painted
a portrait
of his painter
friend
Pechstein
asleep on
a chair
outside.
The picture
dates to 1910.

Picture list

page 4
Jean Dubuffet (1901-1985): *Random Site with Four Figures*, detail, 1982. Paris, Musée National d'Art Moderne. Photo Photothèque des Collections Mnam/Cci. © Jean Dubuffet by SIAE, 1999.

Two ancient Chinese ideograms from the Chou dynasty. 1st millennium B.C.

page 5
Paul Klee (1879-1940): *A Child Again*, pencil drawing, 1939. Bern, Kunstmuseum, Paul-Klee-Stiftung. Museum Photo. © Paul Klee by SIAE, 1999.

page 6
Seated figure carved in a forked branch. Art of the Suku people of the Kwango River area (Zaire). Tervuren, Royal Museum of Central Africa. Drawing by Lorenzo Cecchi.

Top part of a dance staff, from New Britain (Melanesia, Oceania). Private property. Drawing by Lorenzo Cecchi.

page 7
Silhouette of the composer and orchestra conductor Gustav Mahler (1860-1911).

page 8
Crèche figurines in painted terra cotta. Folk art of the Andes Indians, northern Argentina. Madrid, Museum of Decorative Arts. Drawing by Lorenzo Cecchi.

page 9
Iron sculpture of a god of weapons or war, or the divine blacksmith, custodian of the art of iron working. Art of the Yoruba people (Dahomey). Paris, Musée de l'Homme. Drawing by Roberto Simoni.

page 10-11
Anthropomorphic "geoglyph." Nazca civilization, 3rd-4th century A.D. Nazca Pampa (Peru). Drawing by Lorenzo Cecchi.

Figurine in faience of a mummiform ushabti. Egyptian Late Period art, c. 1000-700 B.C. Paris, Louvre. Drawing by Lorenzo Cecchi.

page 12
Votive terra cotta figurine. Sardo-Punic art, 4th-3rd century B.C. Cagliari, Archaeological Museum. Drawing by Lorenzo Cecchi.

Small bronze of an officiating priest. Etruscan art, 3rd century B.C. Rome, Museum of Villa Giulia. Drawing by Lorenzo Cecchi.

page 13
Luca Cambiaso (1527-1585): *Group of Cubic Figures*. Florence, Uffizi, Gabinetto dei Disegni. Photo Scala Archives.

page 14
Leonardo da Vinci (1425-1519): *Scheme of the Proportions of the Human Body*. Venice, Academy. Photo Scala Archives.

page 15
Lyonel Feininger (1871-1956): *The White Man*, 1907. Private property. Photo Scala Archives. © Lyonel Feininger by SIAE, 1999.

page 16
Anavyssos Kouros. Greek art,
6th century B.C. Athens, National
Museum. Photo Scala Archives.

page 17
Diego Velazquez (1599-1660):
The Young Infanta Margarita.
Madrid, Prado. Photo Scala Archives.

page 18
Gypsum statuette of a couple. Sumerian
art, mid 3rd millennium B.C., from Nippur.
Baghdad, Iraq Museum. Drawing
by Roberto Simoni.

page 19
Kasimir Malevich (1878-1935):
Children. Moscow, Pushkin Museum.
Photo Scala Archives.

page 20
Painting of four women running.
Prehistoric rock art, Unbalanja (Australia).
After a copy by Charles P. Mountford.

Giacomo Balla (1871-1958): *Girl Running
on a Balcony*. Milan, Gallery of Modern Art.
Photo Scala Archives. © Giacomo Balla
by SIAE, 1999.

page 21
Auguste Rodin (1840-1917): *The Thinker*.
Paris, Rodin Museum. Photo Scala Archives.

page 22
Niki de Saint Phalle (20th century): *Nana*,
c. 1965. Buffalo, Albright-Knox Art Gallery.

Museum photo. © Niki de Saint Phalle
by SIAE, 1999.

Painting of a dancing female figure.
Prehistoric rock art, 7th millennium B.C.
Tassili-n-Ajjer (Algeria). After a copy
by Jean Dominique Lajoux. Drawing
by Roberto Simoni.

page 23
Giandomenico Tiepolo (1727-1804):
Pulcinella on a Swing. Venice,
Ca' Rezzonico. Photo Scala Archives.

page 24-25
Painting of two people talking.
Prehistoric rock art, 8th millennium B.C.
Ennedi (Chad). After a copy by Gérard Bailloux.
Drawing by Roberto Simoni.

Paul Gauguin (1848-1903): *Ta Matete*
(At the Market). Basle, Kunstmuseum.
Photo Öffentliche Kunstsammlung
Basle / Martin Bühler.

page 26
Terra cotta sculpture known as
Sleeping Lady. 6th millennium B.C.,
from the hypogeum of Hal Saflieni (Malta).
Valletta, National Museum. Drawing by
Lorenzo Cecchi.

page 27
Erich Heckel (1883-1970):
Pechstein Asleep, 1910.
Private property.
Photo Joachim Blauel / Artothek.
© Erich Heckel by SIAE, 1999.